CONTENTS

When you see a 💀, hold the book under a light source for thirty seconds. Then turn off the lights to see the pages glow!

WELCOME

Welcome to a world where things are not quite as they seem...where strange noises and spooky sightings make you run for cover...where ghosts and ghouls meet creepy creatures and haunt the world's scariest places. There's a whole world of weirdness that may or may not be true: some people don't believe in spooks at all. Are you brave enough to turn the pages and see what's lurking inside?

HALL OF HORRORS

GHOUL

A ghoul is the evil manifestation of a dead person who has not passed on to the other side. They continue their existence in this world, lurking in graveyards, sometimes shapeshifting into an animal to watch with glowing eyes and bared teeth. Many ghouls are said to have a taste for human flesh and satisfy their appetites by feasting on newly buried corpses after the procession of loved ones has left them behind.

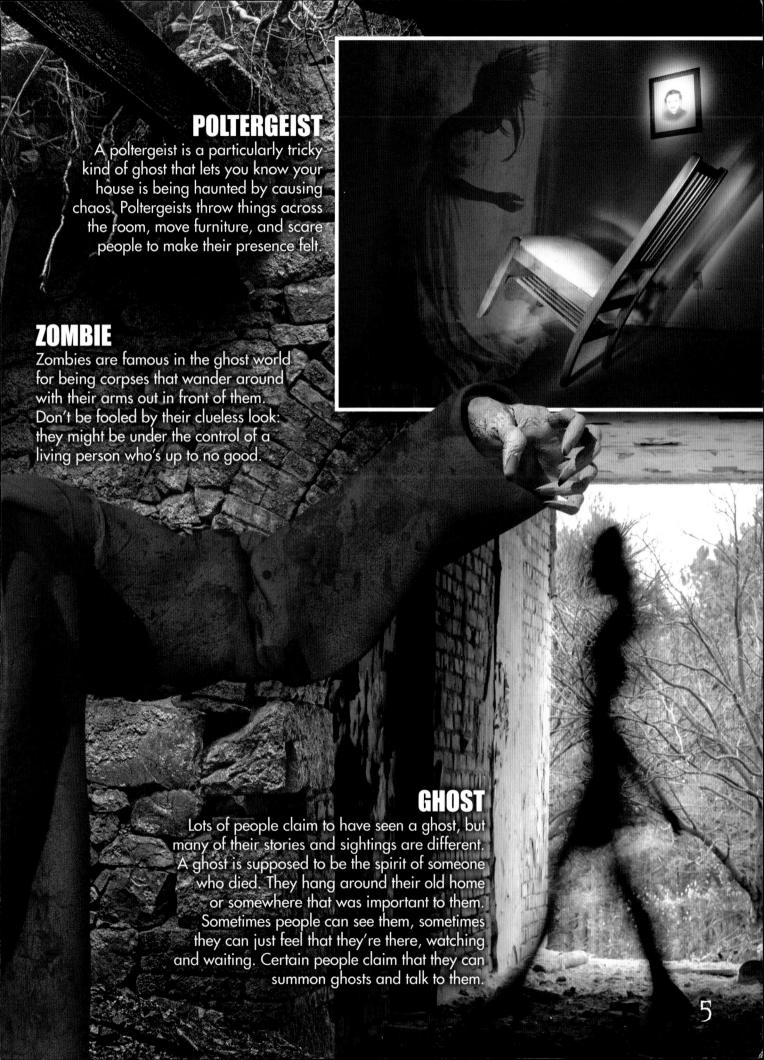

POLTERGEIST

A poltergeist is a particularly tricky kind of ghost that lets you know your house is being haunted by causing chaos. Poltergeists throw things across the room, move furniture, and scare people to make their presence felt.

ZOMBIE

Zombies are famous in the ghost world for being corpses that wander around with their arms out in front of them. Don't be fooled by their clueless look: they might be under the control of a living person who's up to no good.

GHOST

Lots of people claim to have seen a ghost, but many of their stories and sightings are different. A ghost is supposed to be the spirit of someone who died. They hang around their old home or somewhere that was important to them. Sometimes people can see them, sometimes they can just feel that they're there, watching and waiting. Certain people claim that they can summon ghosts and talk to them.

THE GRIM REAPER

This hooded figure is the mascot of Death, cloaked in the black robes of the underworld. He arrives at your side to let you know that your time has come to depart this world. Once the final grains of the sands of life have trickled through his hourglass, he wields his scythe and makes the final cut to sever the soul from its mortal home. Then with a twitch of his skeletal finger, he beckons you to follow him to the other side.

For some, the Grim Reaper is the ultimate portent of doom. His attendance brings the end, and the only way to avoid your fate is by trickery or bribery. For others, this shadowy figure is more of an angel of death, protecting the spirit from harm as he guides it to the afterlife. In this way, the Grim Reaper acts as a "psychopomp," looking after the recently deceased until they find their way. Pyschopomps often take the form of a bird such as a crow, sparrow, or owl, or an animal, most commonly a dog, deer, or horse.

GRAVEYARDS

It is said that the souls of the restless still roam graveyards at night, unable to find peace in this world or the next. From babies and children plucked before their time, to the unfortunates who were badly treated and suffered at the hands of others…they can all choose to come back and seek solace or revenge.

ST. LOUIS CEMETERY

These particular Cities of the Dead are home to the deceased of New Orleans, Louisiana—but with a twist. The bodies are not buried below ground, but have been laid to rest above the earth—making it easier, perhaps, to wander free in the hours of darkness?

GREYFRIARS KIRKYARD IN EDINBURGH

Often called the most haunted graveyard in the world, this burial ground is nestled in the heart of Edinburgh, Scotland. Haunting the cemetery is George MacKenzie, a ruthless official known for the mistreatment and death of hundreds of revolutionaries. His poltergeist is said to roam the cemetery grounds, terrifying and even attacking visitors. Also said to haunt Greyfriars is Bobby, the loyal terrier that stood guard at the grave of his beloved owner John Gray for 14 years until his own death. He was buried in the cemetery close to his master.

HIGHGATE CEMETERY, LONDON

A tranquil setting by day, this burial ground is transformed into a spooky wilderness at night. Home to over 50,000 graves, its spooky setting enticed cultish groups to meet at midnight, calling forth restless souls among the abandoned headstones. Ghostly cyclists, hideous red-eyed creatures, shrouded figures, and a crazy lady looking for her lost children have all spooked the living daylights out of visitors. The grounds even have their own vampire, a tall, menacing, gothic gentleman with piercing eyes and an icy cold aura that chills the air around him.

VAMPIRES

Do you believe in vampires—the undead that return in the black of night to suck the blood of the living? Hundreds of years ago, most people did, and would send vampire hunters to pierce the heart of a corpse to prevent it from harming their loved ones.

VAMPIRE BATS

Nature has its own real-life blood suckers: vampire bats. Named after the literary character, they too emerge after night falls to feast on blood. They do not, however, terrorize humans in their beds, or cause their victims eternal damnation. Vampire bats prey on large farm animals such as goats, cows, and horses, and have highly developed heat sensors to detect their victims in the dark. Their razor sharp teeth graze the flesh until it oozes blood, which they lap up with their tongue. There have been reported cases of humans being bitten by vampire bats, and some people even die of infections such as rabies, but human attacks are rare.

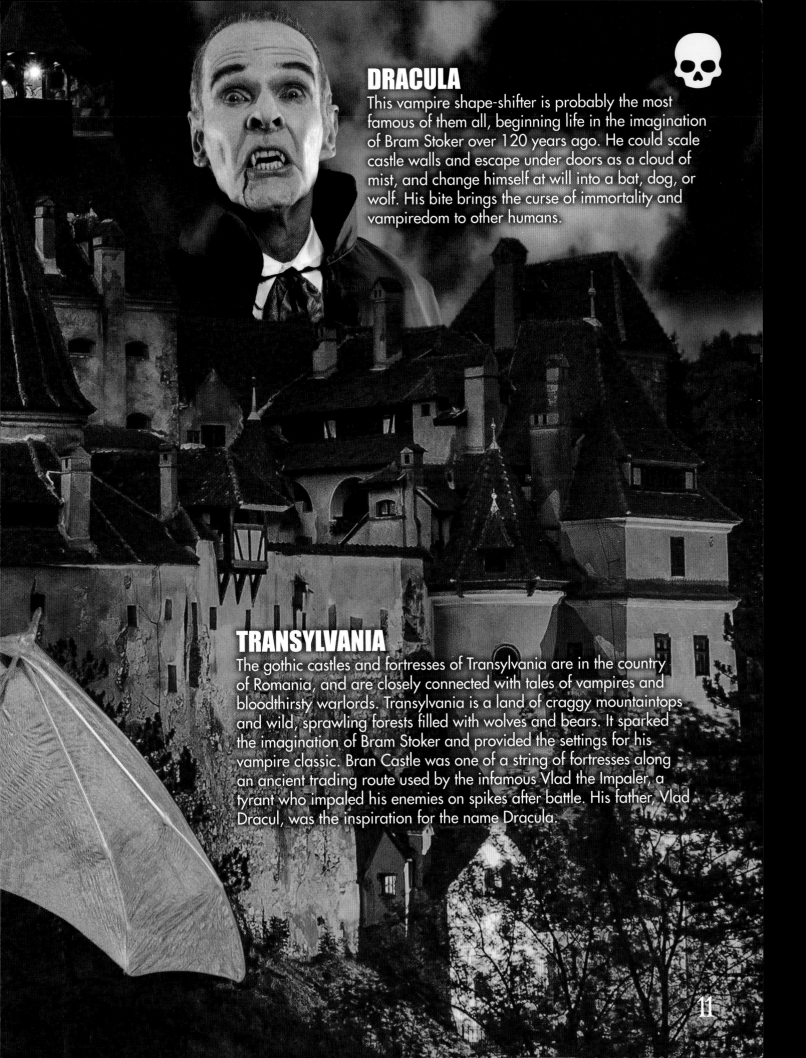

DRACULA

This vampire shape-shifter is probably the most famous of them all, beginning life in the imagination of Bram Stoker over 120 years ago. He could scale castle walls and escape under doors as a cloud of mist, and change himself at will into a bat, dog, or wolf. His bite brings the curse of immortality and vampiredom to other humans.

TRANSYLVANIA

The gothic castles and fortresses of Transylvania are in the country of Romania, and are closely connected with tales of vampires and bloodthirsty warlords. Transylvania is a land of craggy mountaintops and wild, sprawling forests filled with wolves and bears. It sparked the imagination of Bram Stoker and provided the settings for his vampire classic. Bran Castle was one of a string of fortresses along an ancient trading route used by the infamous Vlad the Impaler, a tyrant who impaled his enemies on spikes after battle. His father, Vlad Dracul, was the inspiration for the name Dracula.

MONSTROUS

No matter where you live or where you travel, there will always be a monster myth to spook and unsettle you. Local monsters have the added fear factor of being based in locations you know and probably see every week, but these ghastly creatures from around the world might also give you the jitters.

BIGFOOT

The monstrous hairy beast that is Bigfoot is also known as Sasquatch, and is sighted in remote forests and swamps in North America. Said to look more apelike than human, it is up to twice as tall as a man, with a hairy body and giant hands and feet—hence the nickname. In Asia, a similar creature roams the icy plains and mountains, and is named the Yeti.

BOGEYMAN

Who or what is the bogeyman? Basically, it's pretty much whatever you fear the most…as it's usually the invention of desperate parents who want to frighten their children into staying in bed or doing as they're told. The bogeyman comes in all shapes and sizes, but can see into your room and ALWAYS knows when you're doing something you shouldn't…

WEREWOLVES

A werewolf suffers with an affliction like no other. He is cursed to live as a man for the most part, but uncontrollably takes the form of a wolf at the time of a full moon. Once transformed, werewolves become filled with rage and an overpowering hunger for flesh. They may kill their nearest and dearest, but as they transform back to a human they invariably cannot even remember the horrors they have performed.

CHUPACABRA

Sightings of this wild-eyed beast were first reported in Puerto Rico, and its taste for animal blood has earned it a name that translates as "goat-sucker." The four-legged monster is canine in appearance, with long claws and vicious teeth, but encounters suggest it is the size of a small bear. Many of its animal victims are found with a triangle of puncture wounds in the neck or chest, and attacks are most common in Central and South America.

SEA MONSTERS

KRAKEN

A legendary sea serpent that haunts icy northern waters, the kraken even strikes fear into the hearts of sturdy sailors and courageous captains. Old seafarers describe its jaws as mighty caverns with teeth like rocks around the edges. The many-headed monster lurks in the ocean depths for days on end, and emerges with the turn of the tide when conditions are stormy and the turbulent waves toss boats into its path.

LOCH NESS MONSTER

Nicknamed Nessie, this aquatic monster is said to inhabit Loch Ness in the Scottish Highlands. Over 1,000 sightings have been reported, describing a creature with a long neck and dome-shaped back, much like a plesiosaur. Several photographs have emerged as proof of the monster's existence, but most have been proven to be fakes.

LEVIATHAN

This biblical beast can breathe fire, and the surface of the water boils as it makes its way through the waves. Ruler of all the creatures in the ocean, its eyes gleam and smoke billows from its nostrils.

GIANT SQUID

It was not known until this century whether giant squid were creatures of myth, or whether they really existed. Fishermen told tales of enormous creatures that feasted in the deepest waters, shooting out their tentacles to grab anything tasty in their path. The creatures were up to 60 feet long and powered through the water at high speed. Now scientists have caught specimens to study, and know that they are truly terrifying. They have two tentacles equipped with hundreds of toothed suckers that can seriously harm creatures as large as a whale, and a sharp beak tucked in the middle of their body.

CREEPY CREATURES

DEATH'S HEAD HAWKMOTH

It's not surprising that people have been scared of this creature for centuries. Not only does it come out at night, making a noise in the darkness, but if you see one up close you realize that it has a terrifying skull shape on its back.

PHANTOM DOGS

A wide variety of supernatural dogs occur in mythologies around the world. One such beast is Black Shuck, a huge black ghost dog said to roam the British countryside terrifying anyone in his path. People first notice its glowing red eyes, and then its size; many phantom dogs are as big as a calf, with silent footfalls and a foul smell. Some say that if you stare into the eyes of one of these spectral canines three times, you will die.

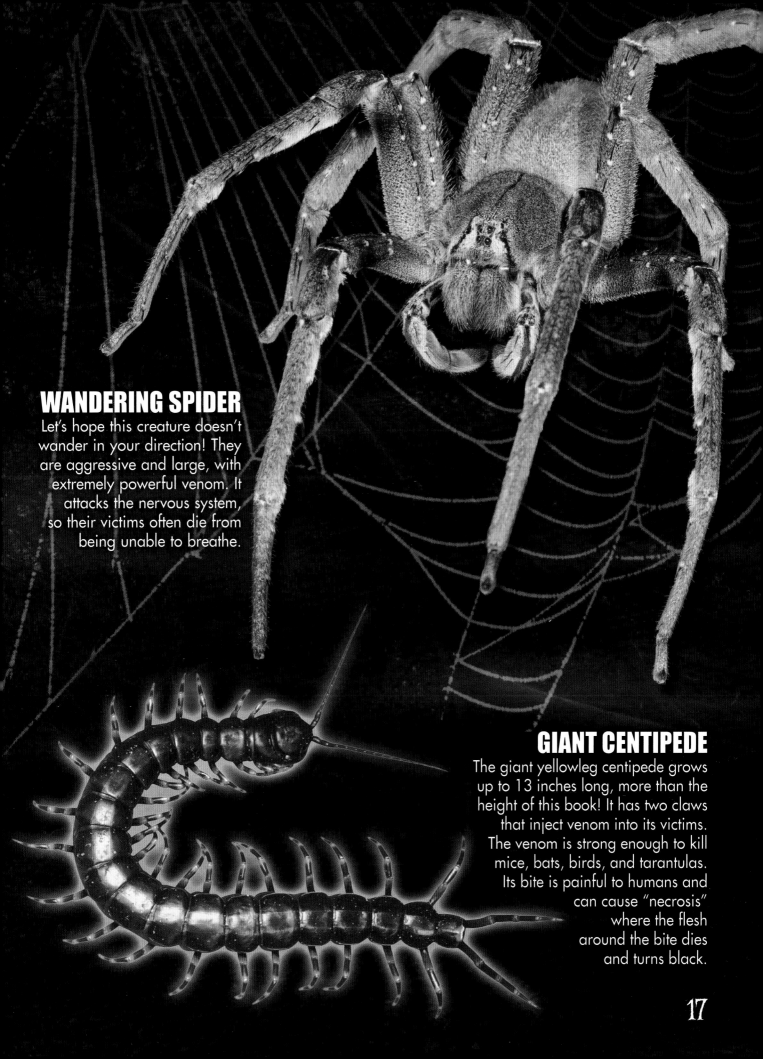

WANDERING SPIDER

Let's hope this creature doesn't wander in your direction! They are aggressive and large, with extremely powerful venom. It attacks the nervous system, so their victims often die from being unable to breathe.

GIANT CENTIPEDE

The giant yellowleg centipede grows up to 13 inches long, more than the height of this book! It has two claws that inject venom into its victims. The venom is strong enough to kill mice, bats, birds, and tarantulas. Its bite is painful to humans and can cause "necrosis" where the flesh around the bite dies and turns black.

17

DRAGONS

EUROPEAN DRAGONS

Commonly portrayed with scaly or bat-like leathery wings, the dragons of European folklore are large, muscular, fire-breathing beasts. They have a set of gigantic talons to grasp prey or enemies and carry them back to their underground lair. This is where many dragons keep their treasure, which they guard day and night, sleeping with one eye open to prevent any intruders stealing their precious hoard.

CHINESE DRAGONS

With a horse's head and a snake's tail, dragons from the East are revered rather than feared. They have supernatural powers, being able to transform into water or clouds and camouflage themselves in any surroundings. If angered, they can release their wrath upon the human world, in the form of floods and tidal waves. Some breathe bursts of fire as a punishment for human wrongdoing.

GEORGE AND THE DRAGON

St. George is the patron saint of several countries, including England, Georgia, and Romania. Legend has it that a dragon lived in a lake on the outskirts of a town, and terrorized the people who lived nearby. They tried to pacify it by feeding it their sheep, and then their children. On the day that their princess was due to be sacrificed, St. George arrived just in time to run his sword through the beast and rescue the princess.

WITCHES

CASTING A SPELL

Folklore tells us that a witch is a wizened old hag who stirs up mischief and malevolence in her cauldron, casting spells and passing poison potions to unsuspecting victims who have done her wrong.

UNDER YOUR SKIN

Ancient witches were described in many forms. Some were wraith-like and insubstantial, but could cause you harm as they muttered incantations under their breath. Others were beautiful, to tempt unsuspecting victims with their charms. The poisonous green skin of many modern witches betrays their inhuman form, and looked especially good on film when the Wicked Witch of the West was first seen in *The Wizard of Oz*.

MORGAN LE FAY

A character from the legends of King Arthur, Morgan le Fay was a powerful enchantress, also known as Morgana. She is a beguiling but evil character who leads heroes into danger with her wily charms and witchcraft. She is able to fly and shapeshift, and can transform her looks to be old or young, beautiful or ugly. She uses her black magic against her half-brother, Arthur.

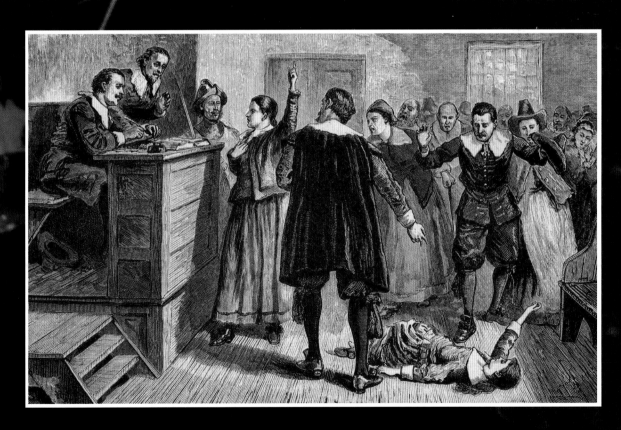

SALEM WITCH TRIALS

Do witches hide away in hovels, or exist among us disguised as ordinary folk? That is what the people of Salem, Massachusetts, suspected in the winter of 1692. Strange happenings in the woods at night led them to believe that the devil was in town, taking possession of women and turning them to witchcraft. Hysteria took hold, and 19 people were tried and hanged as witches, and many more were accused and lived in fear for their lives.

MYTHICAL BEASTS

MEDUSA

Medusa was one of three petrifying Gorgon sisters from Greek mythology. She was a monster in female form, with fangs and claws, staring eyes, and dragon-like scales on her body. She had a headful of writhing, venomous snakes instead of hair. Perhaps most frightening of all, it was said that a look from a Gorgon could turn the onlooker to stone. Two of the sisters were immortal, but Medusa was eventually slain by Perseus, who chopped off her ghastly head.

MINOTAUR

Half-human and half-bull, the Minotaur had an appetite for humans, and was locked away in a labyrinth beneath the royal palace of Crete to keep it out of harm's way. It was fed with human sacrifices until it was eventually slain by Theseus, who then had to find his way out of the labyrinth, after all his efforts.

CERBERUS

A pet dog may be man's best friend, but don't rely on this terrifying beast for companionship. Featured in Greek myth, this Hound of Hades not only has three heads with mouthfuls of vicious fangs, but also has spines, snakes along its body, and a serpent for a tail. According to legend, its father and brothers also had many heads, making them a family to be truly feared.

GHOST STORIES

Every town, every city, every nation has its ghost stories. They are passed down through generations and spread from one area to another. Sometimes they are written down, but often they pass from person to person and generation to generation purely by word of mouth.

BLOODY MARY

Have you ever had that feeling that there's something in the mirror that catches your eye but can't quite be seen? It could be the phantom of Bloody Mary. According to legend, her ghost appears in the mirror when you summon her by calling out her name three times. Who was Bloody Mary? No one knows, some say she may be a witch who lived over 100 years ago.

A CHRISTMAS CAROL

This seasonal tale by Charles Dickens features some of the best-known ghosts in English literature. Four ghosts visit the miserly Ebenezer Scrooge to teach him a lesson. The first is Jacob Marley, warning his former business partner against his greed and selfishness. The ghost of Christmas Past is both young and old, with light streaming from its head. Christmas Present is a jolly ghost, but Christmas Yet to Come is a silent, ominous specter that foretells Scrooge's own miserable death if he doesn't change his ways.

HEADLESS HORSEMAN

This spectral rider appears in tales that are centuries old, across Europe, Asia, and North America. It usually carries its head on its saddle, or held aloft to see farther from its steed. It famously appears in *The Legend of Sleepy Hollow* by American author Washington Irving. Here, the headless ghost rider makes an appearance to poor Ichabod Crane, riding home through the haunted glen at night. The horseman makes chase, and throws its severed head to knock Ichabod from his own horse.

THE LADY IN WHITE

The White Lady is a female ghost figure dressed all in white that appears in legends from around the world. There are several Lady in White legends found throughout the United States like the Lady of the Lake in Rochester, New York. This White Lady apparition wanders a park in search of her deceased daughter.

MAGIC AND MYSTERY

History and fairy tales often meet in a misty place where real people become the stuff of legend. Some stories feature maligned characters who are turned to evil because they are ill-treated by their enemies, while others have supernatural powers that they harness for good.

EVIL QUEEN

The Brothers Grimm used this character in their German fairy tales of the 19th century. She was the wicked stepmother of the gentle Snow White, a girl whom she loathed and ordered to be killed. When her plan didn't work, she transformed herself into an old hag and visited the girl, trying to tempt her into eating poison in a rosy red apple.

26

MALEFICENT

Sometimes known as the Mistress of All Evil, this truly wicked spirit puts a curse on the newborn Princess Aurora, later known as Sleeping Beauty, at her christening. The curse is conjured up out of spite as she was not invited to the celebration, and Maleficent is powerful enough to cast a spell that cannot be broken by any other magic. She transforms herself at will, sometimes into a will-o-the-wisp, or a dark dragon, and also into the spinning wheel that ultimately pricks the princess's finger to make the curse come true.

MERLIN

A wizard serving in the court of King Arthur, Merlin has featured in many legends, poems, and stories. Said to be the greatest sorcerer to ever walk the Earth, his powers were plentiful. He could talk to animals, conjure up spells and potions, and predict the future. His literary life is a jumble of many stories, passed through the ages and combined in people's minds as one great character. In the tales of the Arthurian court, it is Merlin who tutors Morgan le Fay and allows her to become a sorceress of great power.

GHOST TRAIN

TAY BRIDGE DISASTER

A real-life tragedy occurred in Scotland on a stormy night in December 1879. The weather conditions were so bad that a rail bridge collapsed, taking with it an entire train. All 75 passengers were killed…and are said to still haunt the area, returning each year on the anniversary of their death. Their screams can be heard in the night as their carriages plunge into the river below.

ABRAHAM LINCOLN'S GHOST TRAIN

If you feel a distinct chill in the air, then hear a steam train whistle and see steam billowing from an unseen locomotive, this former US President's funeral train may just have passed you by. Each year around the time of the anniversary of Lincoln's death, this train with a skeletal crew, and phantom guards watch over Lincoln's ghostly body in its funeral casket as it winds its way from Washington D.C. to Lincoln's birthplace in Springfield, Illinois. As if that isn't creepy enough, when the train stops at a station, all the clocks stop with it until it pulls away again.

GHOST SHIP

There can be few things more uncanny than an abandoned vessel drifting at sea with no clue as to where the crew have gone, and who might return to claim the ship. And yet, if that ship were to drift straight through another boat like a mysterious ocean fog, that could chill the heart of the boldest seadog…that's why tales of ghost ships are told onshore as well as at sea.

MARY CELESTE

In November 1872, the *Mary Celeste* set sail from New York City. Ten days later, the ship was found drifting off course, with not a crew member on board. Her cargo was intact, her sails were up, the boat was seaworthy, and the crew's belongings were undisturbed. But where had the sailors gone? Not a soul from the ship was ever heard from again, and to this day, nobody knows what happened to them.

DAVY JONES'S LOCKER

No sailor wants to stare into Davy Jones's locker, for it is the resting place of drowned mariners. Referring to the bottom of the sea, shipwrecked vessels and drowned sailors are said to be tossed into Davy Jones's locker.

FLYING DUTCHMAN

If you happen to see a ship glowing with a ghostly light, give it a wide berth, for it may well be the *Flying Dutchman*. Cursed to sail the high seas forever, it can never reach port, and is seen as a bad omen for any seafarers who cross its path. The legend of this ghost ship dates back to the 17th century with reported sightings even today.

HAUNTED PLACES

CATACOMBS, PARIS, FRANCE

Imagine the sight: an underground burial area containing the bones of over six million Parisians from the 1700s. There are undoubtedly some unsettled souls wandering the catacombs, trying to rejoin the spirits of their loved ones from long ago. It is said that the walls of bones will talk to you if you stay too long; the living are certainly not invited to linger...

BODIE, CALIFORNIA

This old mining outpost is a ghost town in every sense. Disused and abandoned after the gold rush died down, the settlement now has its resident ghosts. Childish giggling is heard in empty houses, and guests in the hotel have woken to feel suffocated by a heavy weight pressing down on their chest. The Curse of Bodie is said to fall upon anyone who tries to steal a memento, and they are plagued by bad luck until the stolen item is returned.

BANFF SPRINGS HOTEL, CANADA

Some guests who check in to this hotel never check out... while others get out of there as fast as they can. Beware of room 873, where bloody fingerprints appear on the bathroom mirror and the ghosts of a murdered girl and her mother wake guests with their shrieks. And look out for the Phantom Bride who dances alone after dying here on her wedding night.

EASTERN STATE PENITENTIARY

Possibly America's most haunted building, this former prison is in Philadelphia, Pennsylvania. Now open to the public as a museum, it is common for visitors to see shadowy figures in the cells, and report cold pockets of air in the corridors. The screams of tortured inmates can be heard, voicing their torment and claiming some small revenge for the horrors they endured at the hands of cruel prison guards.

THE BLOODY TOWER

THE TOWER OF LONDON

This historic tower is centuries old and has been used as a prison, but also as a royal castle, a zoo, a treasury, and is currently home to the Crown Jewels of England. The White Tower is the oldest part, dating back to 1066, and the bones of two small children were found here in 1674. Several people were imprisoned and beheaded in the so-called "Bloody Tower," with many more executed on Tower Hill outside its walls. It is no surprise that the castle has more than its fair share of hauntings.

PRINCES IN THE TOWER

In July 1483, Richard III was crowned King of England. He had taken the throne from his 12-year-old nephew, who would have become Edward V had he been allowed to inherit the title of king. Instead, Edward's uncle had the young heir, and his younger brother Richard, thrown into the cells in the Tower of London. They were never seen again, believed to have been murdered. Their voices have been heard laughing on the grounds and their ghosts, dressed in white nightshirts, have been seen in the tower—even appearing on tourist photographs.

ANNE BOLEYN AND HENRY VIII

One of the Tower's most famous ghosts is the apparition of Queen Anne Boleyn, second wife of Henry VIII. Sentenced to death by her husband and executed on the Tower grounds, her ghostly figure roams the Queen's House and Tower's chapel clad in a hood with no head beneath it. The White Tower is home to her husband's suit of armor. Visitors have described how they feel an horrendous crushing sensation when they approach the armor, and others have heard threatening voices even though they are alone.

LADY JANE GREY

The living may like to celebrate their birthdays, but Lady Jane Grey is known for making a ghostly appearance on her death-day! The "Nine Days Queen" was not only disowned by her father and made to relinquish her crown and title, but was imprisoned in the Tower and beheaded on Tower Hill. Hardly surprising, then, that she comes back to haunt her prison, and has been seen many times as a white figure walking along the battlements on the anniversary of her death.

THE WHITE HOUSE

THE WHITE HOUSE, WASHINGTON D.C.

The official home of the President of the United States has many apparitions that lurk in its corridors. Ghosts of former residents, from first ladies to disgruntled and assassinated presidents, have all made their spooky presence felt. Reports include hearing footsteps on the floorboards, and seeing drapes and cushions move.

OVAL OFFICE

The President's official office in the West Wing of the White House is a favorite for several ghosts. President Harry Truman wrote to his wife in 1945 describing the popping of the floors and moving of the drapes as "ghosts walk up and down the hallway and even right here in the study." A disembodied voice claimed to be that of David Burns, the owner of the land on which the White House is built. The most common spectral visitor is Abraham Lincoln, President from 1861 until his assassination in 1865.

LINCOLN BEDROOM

President Abraham Lincoln has reportedly returned to this bedroom in the White House many times. His footsteps sometimes echo in the hall outside, and several guests have heard Lincoln knocking at the door when they stayed in the room. His ghostly figure has been seen perched on the edge of the bed, putting on his boots—one instance of which sent Eleanor Roosevelt's secretary screaming from the room. She wasn't the only staff member to flee in terror; Lincoln's ghost had the same effect on Franklin D. Roosevelt's personal valet who left the White House altogether!

ABRAHAM LINCOLN

Lincoln's ghost is often described as wearing a top hat and coat, but it cares not what its guests are wearing. The British Prime Minister Winston Churchill had just taken a bath and was in a distinct state of undress when the ghost dropped by! Lincoln's ghostly form stood by the fireplace as Churchill reportedly said, "Good evening, Mr. President. You seem to have me at a disadvantage." The ghost smiled and disappeared, but the Prime Minister refused to stay in that room again.

BAD OMENS

HOOTING OWL

Hunters of the night, owls are sacred in many cultures, and guard the souls of the dead. For many people, though, an owl is a bad omen. To dream of an owl was a warning of a death in the family, and a hooting owl was either a call to the underworld or a warning that there was a witch in the area.

TICK TOCK

As you lie in bed late at night, take careful note of the chiming of the clock. After twelve midnight, you may hear a thirteenth strike. It brings bad news: it foretells the death of the youngest member of the household.

HOLD YOUR BREATH

Be very careful if you walk through a graveyard, for many fates await the unwary. Never take flowers from a grave, or its spirit will haunt you. Hold your breath as you pass the gravestones to prevent evil spirits entering your body.

BLACK CATS

Many witches take the form of a black cat, or keep one as their familiar: an animal-shaped demon that serves her evil pursuits. If a black cat walks away from you, it will take good luck with it. And never let a black cat lie on your bed, or you may not wake in the morning…

MUMMY

The Ancient Egyptians are well-known for preserving the bodies of their important figures to see them into the afterlife. Other cultures also prepared their dead, from a Chinchorro child found in Chile to severed, shrunken heads in the Amazon rainforest.

NAZCA MUMMY

The Nazca people of Peru also mummified their dead to preserve them for the afterlife, but their remains were disturbed from their peace by grave robbers at the Chauchilla Cemetery. The ninth-century bodies had been clothed and then painted with a special resin to stop them being eaten by insects; many of the mummies still have patches of hair and skin.

MUMMY'S CURSE

It is said that the curse of the Pharaohs will follow anyone who disturbs the ancient tombs of Egyptian rulers, whether they stumble upon them by accident, for research, or with bad intent. The tomb of Tutankhamun lay undiscovered and undisturbed for centuries, until it was opened by Egyptologist Howard Carter in 1922. A series of deaths after it was explored led people to believe that the tomb was indeed cursed, and that ill health and misfortune would accompany anyone who had played a part in disturbing the tomb.

ALL HALLOWS' EVE

ALL SAINTS

You probably know this celebration better as Halloween, or maybe even All Saints' Eve, and it takes place on October 31. It is the first part of a three-day celebration called Allhallowtide, running into November 1 and 2. People gather to remember the deceased: from saints and martyrs to loved ones who are no longer alive. The festival has ancient roots, dating back hundreds of years to Samhain, a Celtic custom when people dressed in animal skins to frighten away any unwanted spirits. They believed that Samhain was the time when the dead returned to Earth, lit bonfires, and offered food and even sacrifices to keep the deceased happy.

TRICK OR TREAT?

In many countries nowadays, particularly the US and UK, children visit their neighbors' houses to collect candy and food treats. You may think it is a new activity, but it bears similarities to the thousand-year-old tradition of "souling" where children would visit houses to ask for soul cakes in return for prayers for the homeowners' dead relatives. Celtic children (in Scotland, Ireland, and parts of France) also took part in "guising" which involved dressing up and performing a "trick" such as a joke or a song to receive a treat. Sound familiar?

JACK-O-LANTERN

Halloween costumes come in varying degrees of scariness, and so do jack-o-lanterns. Some are pumpkin works of art, many are grinning faces with uneven teeth, but some stare creepily out from your neighbor's porch. The tradition began in Ireland with potato and turnip carving, and was carried across the Atlantic to the US where pumpkins were in abundance. They are said to look like a will o' the wisp or jack o' lantern—a natural but spooky light that flickers over bogs and marshes. The lanterns were placed in homes at Samhain to keep away any evil spirits.

HALLOWEEN

43

CLOWN FINGERS

Have you heard the story about Molly's dolly? The little girl in question begged her mother to buy her a clown doll that was mysteriously holding up three fingers. The shopkeeper warned her not to leave her daughter alone with the creepy toy. Molly played happily with the doll all afternoon, until her mother tucked her up in bed. The next morning, Molly was gone, and all that remained was the doll…which was now holding up four fingers.

ROBERT THE DOLL

On display at the East Martello Museum in Key West, Florida, Robert the Doll is said to be cursed with a life of its own. It was a gift from a servant who dabbled in black magic, presented to Robert Eugene Otto when he was a child. The doll seemed to come alive, moving from room to room when no-one was home, and talking to the young boy when he played with it.

ISLAND OF THE DOLLS

It takes a brave soul to visit the Isla de las Muñecas, or Island of the Dolls, just south of Mexico City. It is inhabited by hundreds of dolls with staring eyes and missing limbs; the locals swear that those with arms and legs move them around, and those that aren't headless whisper to each other. Legend tells us that they are possessed by the spirit of a young girl who drowned in the water around the island. Some even say that they have heard the dolls calling to them as they sail close by, trying to lure them to the haunted place.

VOODOO DOLLS

It is said that black magic can be used with these effigies, or likenesses of real people, to inflict pain upon the human they represent. Believers will name a doll and sometimes mark it with a hair from the chosen victim, and then stick pins into it to cause that person harm. The practice began centuries ago, when dolls were made to symbolize a suspected witch and pins poked in to undo their spells and enchantments.

45

DAY OF THE DEAD

THE DANCE OF DEATH

The *Día de los Muertos* is a public holiday in Mexico and a celebration throughout Central America, held to praise and honor the dead. The celebrations include processions, parties, and feasts, and take place on All Saints' Day (November 1) and All Souls' Day (November 2). People want to be happy about the lives of their loved ones, instead of being sad about their death, which is seen as insulting to those who have passed away.

GIFTS TO THE DEAD

Local people believe that the gates of heaven open at midnight on October 31. Then the spirits of *angelitos*, or children who have passed away, are reunited with their families for a day of celebrations. Altars are decorated with *pan de muerto*, Day of the Dead bread, and treats such as soda, cocoa, candies, and toys. Sugar skulls and carved skeletons called *calacas* decorate the altars.

AROUND THE WORLD

Different countries have their own rituals for celebrating life and death. The Day of the Dead is not only celebrated in Mexico, but also in Spain, Italy, the Philippines, and South America. As well as paying their respects and reminiscing about their loved ones, people pray for their souls, and tidy and clean their tombs. In Bolivia on November 8 they go even further with the Day of the Skull, when real human skulls, handed down through families, are dressed in hats and sunglasses or decorated with flowers and put on display.

REAL LIFE MONSTERS

IVAN THE TERRIBLE

The first Tsar of Russia, Ivan was a warlord and tyrant who had his own people tortured and killed. He ordered the execution of entire families during a period known as the "Oprichnina" when his national guard were ordered to cleanse the country of anyone who challenged the Tsar's authority. It seems he took great delight in making people suffer, and personally led a charge on the city of Novgorod, helping to slaughter thousands of people with his sword.

GENGHIS KHAN

A Mongolian ruler, Genghis Khan built a huge empire across Asia, uniting countries into one military state. He ruled this state through tyranny and fear, plundering villages and murdering their leaders to ensure nobody would challenge his power. Born in the middle of the 12th century and given the name Temujin, legend told that he was a divine being, with gray wolves as his ancestors.